THEATRE YEAR

A selection of photographs by Donald Cooper of productions in London and Stratford September 1983 to October 1984.

With an introduction and index by Michael Coveney.

In (Parenthesis) Limited

Front cover, from left to right:
Starlight Express (Apollo Victoria)   Stephanie Lawrence *Pearl*; Ray Shell *Rusty*
42nd Street (Theatre Royal, Drury Lane)   Clare Leach *Peggy Sawyer*
On Your Toes (Palace)   Natalia Makarova *Vera Baronova*
West Side Story (Her Majesty's)   Lee Robinson *Anita*

Back cover:
Abbacadabra (Lyric Hammersmith)   Elaine Paige *Carabosse*
Jean Seberg (Olivier)   Kelly Hunter *Young Jean*
The Mikado (Old Vic)   Richard McMillan *Pooh-Bah*
Poppy (Adelphi)   Antonia Ellis *Dick Whittington*

The dates listed refer to the official Press nights. Every
effort has been made to ensure the accuracy of the
information given.

Published by In (Parenthesis) Limited
21 Wellington Street, London WC2

Photographs Copyright ©Donald Cooper 1983/1984

Introduction and Production Notes Copyright ©Michael Coveney 1984

Printed in England by
Battley Brothers Printers, Clapham, London SW4 0JN
Cover designed by Ted Sawtell

Introduction

By Michael Coveney,
theatre critic of the Financial Times.

The gloom and doom of two years ago seemed to be thoroughly dispelled for most of the period covered by this report. London theatre attendance is reckoned to have increased by 10% in 1984, but this statistic is dangerously dependent on the continuing strength of the dollar and the consequent flood of our good friends the American tourists.

There was an endless procession of major musical productions beginning ominously with *Blondel* (rhyming with 'fondle'), *Jean Seberg* and *Dear Anyone*, and stretching out more confidently to *Starlight Express, On Your Toes* and *42nd Street*. But still no West End home was found for the National Theatre's 1982 *Guys and Dolls*, revived on the South Bank with Bernard Cribbins a splendid new Nathan Detroit.

Actors bustled and thrived all year, not only in the public view but also behind the scenes, where they were busy forming new patterns and conditions of employment. Ray Cooney's Theatre of Comedy gang, based at the Shaftesbury, consolidated a good first year with a hugely successful revival of the classic farce *See How They Run* which, even though it was by no means faultless, was considerably better than the Royal Shakespeare Company's unhappy riposte in the Babican with *The Happiest Days of Your Life*.

The other Theatre of Comedy success was *Loot* in which Leonard Rossiter gave his last performance as a maniacally inspired Truscott of the Yard in a superb production by Jonathan Lynn. Some critics surprisingly felt that Orton's gorgeously profane impact was on the wane. No more than is Marlowe's, Jonson's or Coward's, I reckon.

United British Artists was a brand new alignment claiming the support of Diana Rigg, Maggie Smith, Glenda Jackson, Richard Johnson, Albert Finney and other stars for whom stage work may prove a plausible luxury if tied in with the economic rewards of television and film deals. UBA opened with *The Biko Inquest* at Riverside Studios (31 1 84), Finney directing and appearing in an unelaborated documentary about the mysterious death in prison of a black South African civil rights leader.

Finney confirmed the suspicion that he was no threat to Orson Welles as an actor-cum-director by repeating the double function in a lacklustre revival of *Serjeant Musgrave's Dance* at the gloriously refurbished Old Vic. The best of UBA ironically implicated none of their star names, as Lindsay Anderson brought his glowing Edinburgh Festival production of *The Playboy of the Western World* to London.

Interesting formations, too, at the Royal Court where the Women's Playhouse Trust, which aims to redress an alleged sexual imbalance of power in the theatre, spluttered rather than sprang into life with Aphra Behn's *The Lucky Chance*; and at Greenwich, where Philip Prowse of the Glasgow Citizens' supervised a three-play season of Webster, Congreve and Chekhov.

In the Webster, Gerard Murphy took the stage as Brachiano and promptly vomited onto the floor, reminding one of what Barry Humphries used to get up to on aeroplanes with diced vegetables. Earlier at Stratford East he had played an insouciant, well-spoken Pericles. But it was Murphy's third major role of the year that deservedly earned him undiluted critical applause. He played the Renaissance army captain Goetz in Sartre's *The Devil and the Good Lord* with such headlong bravery and contagious ferocity that he fully compensated for an otherwise neutral production by John Dexter of a fitfully tedious (when Murphy was off) five-hour existentialist epic. Murphy has been a notable Glasgow Macbeth, an underrated RSC Prince Hal. This performance, undoubtedly, was the breakthrough.

There were many other outstanding feats in an altogether remark-able year for acting. Frances Barber brought off a superb triple jump to stardom as a tentative PA in a Bush Theatre comedy about filming in India, as a plangently consumptive Camille in the RSC's Other Place, and as Roger Rees's deeply touching, affectionate and spurned Ophelia on the Stratford main stage. Also at Stratford-upon-Avon, Kenneth Branagh confirmed everything he promised in *Another Country* as a vibrant, tough and sympathetic young Henry V, followed by lower pitched but equally impressive appearances as Laertes and the King of Navarre. Simon Callow weighed in with an exhaustingly extravagant double shuffle as a Hammersmith Lord Foppington – Vanbrugh's vowels have never been so accurately nor so gloriously relished – and a Watford Tony Perelli. These palpably contrived but irresistible displays were nonetheless solo turns which made one worry a little about Callow's call for Actors' Lib at the expense of directors' control in his remarkable, honest and well-written book *Being an Actor*.

The RSC at Stratford was again in the hands of the younger directors. The post-Priestley Report liberated mood of scenographic luxuriance prevails. The team of Adrian Noble and Bob Crowley flourishes in this climate. Their resplendent Age of Reason *Measure* established Juliet Stevenson as the RSC's best young actress in worthy succession to Ashcroft and Dench, and their absolutely stunning *Henry V* benefited from being treated, scene by scene, on its own internal merits and not as a coda to the Prince Hal plays in a sequence of Histories, which is how I remember the previous RSC Henrys of Ian Holm and Alan Howard.

Doubts began to settle later in the season over Ron Daniels's *Hamlet* and Barry Kyle's *Love's Labour's Lost*. Neither director is a naturally gifted visual artist of the stage. Their talents lie elsewhere. *Hamlet*, with its awkwardly organised perspex balustrades and echoing staircases, and *Love's Labour's* with its emphatic echoes of films like *Last Year at Marienbad* and *Jules et Jim* – both shows camouflaged textually weak all-round work in ambitious but shakily unconvincing design gestures.

Still, Roger Rees, recovering from a bad performance in *Cries from the Mammal House* at the Royal Court, was a fine, neurasthenic Hamlet with a Bedlamite, Poor Tom streak of coruscatingly witty madness. He was also an alert Berowne although hectic mannerism crept into the comic playing.

The problem for the RSC, one which never goes away, is how can Shakespeare be truthfully animated year in, year out, without merely tarting up the texts in a high-gloss finish. Passion and impulse yielding an urgent contemporaneity can only be stirred by asking the question 'Why do this play *now*?' and then stripping off the old flakey layers of paint to apply fresh undercoat.

Richard III is a bit different. It stands or falls by its central performance and, with Antony Sher, it most certainly stood. Sher was simply sensational. No English actor since Olivier has really claimed the role as his own, but Sher did just that. Bill Alexander's production considerably provided an emblematic Gothic framework of competent support, cathedral plasterwork and a few tombs. Sher did the rest. He was candescent, speedy, viperish, sinking into a great wash of lassitude on the eve of Bosworth Field.

Every foul description thrown at Richard was returned in mesmerically physical kind, Sher rattling and scooting around the stage on his black medical crutches, one minute an unbottled spider, the next a hunch-backed toad, now a beetle, now a hovering bat. Above all, though, this was a study in the crude exploitation of disability, for Sher's Richard was a different sort of cripple, a different *power* of invalid, to different people. No-one really knew where they were with him. But the moment he achieved the crown, the spirit drained away, the props, the crutches, were discarded. The point was made that, having gained ultimate authority, Richard had not a clue as to how he should use it.

The production was one of two this year to make excellent use of interval placement (the *Hamlet* break was unaccountably taken in the middle of the night sequence which runs continuously from the play scene through the closet to Hamlet's banishment). *Richard III* drove on to the coronation, culminating in an RSC pageant where we saw Richard's 'real' hump in a ceremonial blessing and where the avenging ghosts were already gathering. At Greenwich, Philip Prowse placed his *Seagull* interval after the third act, thereby underlining the two-year passage of time and reaping all sorts of character rewards.

At the Barbican, *The Happiest Days* was deprived of one interval, thus upsetting the three-act structure, an error also perpetrated by the Haymarket revival of *The Aspern Papers* in which Vanessa Redgrave and Wendy Hiller (complete with bath chair and tennis umpire's peaked cap) gave magical performances, the one fanned to translucent life by the arrival of Christopher Reeve, the other huskily crotchety in her denial of Miss Redgrave's last chance to break free. At the National, neither *Jean Seberg* nor *Mandragola* had an interval, but that was merely because no-one would have bothered to return from the bar had one been provided.

It was indeed a modest year at the National. The fuss over *Seberg* soon died down when the show was revealed to be neither very good nor very bad. Michael Pennington was compellingly tormented in *Strider* and *Venice Preserv'd*, and none too happy as a strangely pernickety Anton Chekhov (the only other notable one-man show was Alec McCowen's acclaimed tour de force as Kipling, which moved from the Mermaid (31 5 84) to New York in October). Ian McKellen was impressive, too, in the Otway, but he really hit the front as Platonov in Michael Frayn's wonderfully farcical reclamation of Chekhov's early unfinished work.

The design for *Wild Honey* was lavish: a silver birch forest à la Peter Stein's *Summerfolk*, a functional train looming from the dark recesses of the country night, a cottage by the railway line in the woods. Frayn's achievement was to give us a familiar new Chekhov and a brand new farce, full of delightfully funny lines (climactically, 'Your estate, your wife, your revolver – can't you keep your hands on anything?'). McKellen's stunning switches between gregariousness and alcoholic melancholy were behavioural symptoms of the character's inability either to explain himself or stop hurting those closest to him.

Wild Honey and, to a lesser extent, John Mortimer's new Feydeau translation, of the messily titled *A Little Hotel on the Side* – Graeme Garden, though funny, lacked the technical and emotional resonance to suggest true panic or pain – were the NT highlights. *Saint Joan* was a worthy, processional sort of evening in the company of a play I find it increasingly difficult to take all that seriously. Best forgotten is the amnesiac attack suffered by the distinguished actor playing the Inquisitor in the trial scene. Would she go to the stake, would he remember his lines? Not to be outdone, the RSC reserved an even more spectacular memory failure for *The Happiest Days* first night.

Animal Farm did not really explain itself as a production except as the National's nod towards the inevitable Orwellian brouhaha. And the *débâcle* of *Mandragola* was a sorry upshot of the brusque importation from the Southampton Nuffield of director David Gilmore and his talented colleagues Roger Glossop and Howard Goodall. The trio said farewell to Southampton with an ambitious, if flawed, musical version of Melvyn Bragg's *The Hired Man* which later surfaced in London at the Astoria (31 10 84).

The National had a far greater success with Mamet's *Glengarry Glen Ross* than with Shepard's *Fool for Love*. The reason, I suspect, is that Mamet's language is an artefact, a brilliantly stylised commodity which finds a quick response in English actors' talents of articulation, inflection, phrasing and rhythm. On the other hand, Shepard's brutally raw poetic writing needs nothing so much as unadulterated guts, concentrated fury and unequivocal American realism. Anyway, Bill Bryden's team of loyally resilient survivors led us inexorably, fascinatingly, into the labyrinthine treats of Mamet's linguistic invention. The same crew were less convincing in *Golden Boy*, Bryden's deft and telling touch for once deserting him. The sets were impressive but cumbersome, and there were a few dead areas in the casting.

If you don't count *Wild Honey* (I might be tempted to), the two major subsidised companies threw up only one major new play between them, David Edgar's *Maydays* at the Barbican. This was a lament for the politicised hippie generation, and Edgar followed the blueprint of Howard Brenton's 1976 *Weapons of Happiness* in contrasting the comic fate of student Trotskyite Martin Glass with the less comic tale of a dissident Russian officer, Lermontov, who is thrown into a labour camp and arrives in England to be adopted as an anti-Soviet emblem (Solzhenitzyn style) by the British Right. Glass himself has moved, not all that convincingly, into the Establishment and is finally seen expelling Greenham Common women from his patch of property by the US air base.

Edgar's analysis of political shifts to right and left was riveting, beautifully realised in large-scale scenes ranging across Europe even to California, and in well-observed close-up interludes at an Islington cell of the late 1960s splintering Left and at Martin's vicarage home. Anthony Sher was restrained and effective as Martin and Ron Daniels' very fine production, which proved gratifyingly popular at the Barbican, also contained top class work from Bob Peck as the dissident who just stopped the political exploitation rot in a memorable official dinner scene, and from John Shrapnel as Martin's academic and philosophical guru in whose defection from the Communist Party after the invasion of Hungary was encapsulated the political schizophrenia inevitably found among sensibly sceptical British left-wingers.

The theatre, perhaps as usual, found it difficult to engage with the ghastly realities of life and there was – how could there be? – no answer to the IRA bombing of the Brighton hotel where the Prime Minister and her Cabinet colleagues were lucky to survive. Shortly after that obscenity, the Royal Court offered a play about sexual high jinks among Tory politicians, *An Honourable Trade*. Unlucky, this, for the last Tory politician to be seen wearing pyjamas on the BBC Television News was Norman Tebbit being dug out of the hotel rubble after several hours of painful incarceration.

An Irish season at the Royal Court featured Ron Hutchinson's *Rat in the Skull*, an objectively written confrontation between an Ulster policeman and an IRA suspect, and the much more theatrically impressive *Up to the Sun and Down to the Centre* by Peter Cox in the Theatre Upstairs (10 9 84). The latter came out of a research trip to republican strongholds in Belfast, but despite some naïve international socialist guff, it quite transcended the purposeful conditions of composition and took off as a funny, rich and poetic play about the contemporary troubles as they infect family life.

The Royal Court is under threat from the Arts Council, who intend to withdraw the grant to the English Stage Company unless there are signs over the next couple of years of support from the local borough council. This ridiculous and irresponsible Arts Council posture is akin to them arguing for closure of the RSC in Stratford unless the equally surly and ungrateful local council suddenly and miraculously starts to support the company which brings such prosperity to the neighbourhood.

With those Irish plays, and with Michael Hastings's brilliantly presented and acted version of T S Eliot's first marriage, *Tom and Viv*, the Court, under the admittedly entrenched artistic directorship of Max Stafford-Clark, more than earned its keep. Thirty years after the breakthrough of Osborne, Pinter and Beckett, it is astonishing that only one major British theatre is unflinchingly dedicated to new writing. To threaten its existence is scandalous, unforgiveable.

However, one of the Court's current weaknesses is that it rarely breaks the mould or surprises very much with its obsessions or tone. Nor does it seem to attract star actors any more. As regards writers, under William Gaskill, say, the careers of such disparate talents as Hampton, Storey and Bond were simultaneously developed. One wonders if the Royal Court ever tries to woo people like Willy Russell, John McGrath or David Pownall with as much dedication as it lends to the promulgation of youth theatre and school-play projects.

Pownall's *Master Class* arrived at the Old Vic after a Leicester première. Once it got going, this was a superbly theatrical discussion of artistic licence and censorship under Stalin, superbly played by

Timothy West, with Peter Kelly and David Bamber a brilliantly contrasted pair of piano-playing composers, Prokofiev and Shostakovich. The record-crunching scene was one of the year's high-lights and a wonderful excuse for Mr West to unleash his talent for the expression of horribly intimidating physical anger.

Manneristic comedy flourished in the not too dissimilar worlds of Doug Lucies's *Progress* at the Bush and, opening on the very next night, Simon Gray's *The Common Pursuit* at Hammersmith. Gray's elegy for lost aspirations among an Oxbridge literary coterie smacked a little of incestuous nit-picking and failed to transfer to Shaftesbury Avenue. It was directed, cunningly, by Harold Pinter who had fallen in the with the UBA after falling out with Peter Hall over National Theatre policy and a few lines to which he took exception in the already notorious Hall Diaries. The Hammersmith studio thus found itself with a Pinter première, *On the Road*, in which Alan Bates gave an inimitably nasty and powerful performance for a miniscule lunchtime audience.

It was a very dry year until mid-September, but musicals poured down on the capital in a glistening spring, then summer, rain. The orchestrations and musical direction of both *On Your Toes* and *42nd Street* were fabulous, beyond praise. Two young American artists were rapturously received by London audiences: Tim Flavin, devastatingly gifted and sympathetic as a partner first to Makarova then to Panova in *On Your Toes*, and Clare Leach as Peggy Sawyer, the understudy in *42nd Street* who goes out there a youngster and comes back, natch, a star.

Without Jerry Orbach's New York performance as the Svengali producer, *42nd Street* had a gaping hole in its heart, and the designs and costumes struck me, second time around, as crude and raucous. Removed from its Broadway hothouse natural environment, the show wilted rather more than somewhat. The tap dancing was reasonably good, but the choreography was simply arch when compared with the innovative, still astonishing work of Balanchine, Donald Saddler and George Abbott (the sprightliest 97-year-old in the business) in *On Your Toes*.

Andrew Lloyd Webber's *Starlight Express* attracted praise and contempt by the bucketful, inevitably perhaps for a show which fell between the two stools of environmental theatricality and mundane narrative imperatives. The opening ten minutes of pulsatingly anticipatory rock and Spielbergian mystery in a celestial train shed were as sensuously magical as anything I have experienced in a theatre. The first half was, in fact, more or less spellbinding. This was *Cats* Mark II with a touch of Disneyland and *The Wizard of Oz*.

It was, at the very least, refreshing to see all these elements of contemporary culture employed by the theatre in the way that Brecht used to vandalise and appropriate the popular song and cabaret styles of *his* time. It would be crass to deny the experimental goodwill lurking behind *Starlight*, even if the show was, as one critic put it, a millionaire's bauble that happened to be on display to the public. The choreography reflected the street-dance culture of body popping, roller skating and robotic variations, even if it did run out of steam.

You could say that the celebration of the steam engine and old values was a little arch in a show that depended so obviously on technological and sophisticated theatrical weaponry. You could also say that this was the ironic point behind it all. Or else, if you were aged between six and sixteen, you could just enjoy the evening.

Harking back to structure, it was a good year for architects and planners. In the NT Feydeau, a building contractor attempted to exact adulterous revenge on his architect neighbour. Two Michael Codron productions, the Hampstead transfer of Stephen Fagan's *The Hard Shoulder* and the Vaudeville Theatre (which Codron now owns) presentation of Michael Frayn's *Benefactors*, discussed sexual and professional angst among the designers of the modern urban landscape. I was unable to echo the euphoria over *Benefactors* (best play for years said some, ho hum) but willing to acknowledge the piquancy of its limited, Ibsenite appeal. The writing was sharp, but the format, using flashback and direct address, stale and unexciting.

I cried with laughter twice as I remember: at Rossiter's *Loot* and during a couple of scenes of *Volpone* at the RSC's Other Place in Stratford, where Bruce Alexander's Sir Politic Would-Be listed his hare-brained schemes and plots with a view to making a name and a fortune. It was the Other Place's tenth anniversary season, an occasion most happily marked by Louise Page's *Golden Girls*, a timely play about women athletes – the sexual, competitive and sponsorship pressures – brilliantly directed by Barry Kyle, and by a darting, vivacious Juliet from Amanda Root.

For the record, written not pictorial, there were four blazingly awful London first nights: *The Importance* at the Ambassadors (31 5 84), a musical version of Wilde with one of many terrible songs called 'Born in a Handbag'; *Corpse!* at the Apollo (26 7 84) which, like *Twang!* and *Marilyn!* had an indefensible exclamation mark; *Big in Brazil* at the Old Vic (19 9 84), a farcical fiasco notable only for reuniting on stage the husband and wife team of Timothy West and the delightful Prunella Scales; and the truly execrable *Top People*, again at the Ambassadors (11 10 84), by the forlorn *Rocky Horror Show* author Richard O'Brien. Only *Corpse!*, oddly enough, survived. It was, so they said, a thriller, but not a patch on *Sleuth* which it very faintly resembled.

Strange Interlude, with exceptional support work from Edward Petherbridge, Brian Cox and James Hazeldine, was my favourite show of the year. It was a second triumphant success for Glenda Jackson, director Keith Hack, designer Voytek and producing mangement Triumph Apollo in the wake of last year's *Great and Small*. The play's experimental, even gauche, use of interior monologue was ingeniously turned to stylistic advantage. And I loved the way Jackson and Hack transformed a play which began in O'Neill's present and ended, five hours later, in a future he could only guess at (no Second World War!), into a consistently emotional and presentational whole.

Glenda Jackson followed this truly remarkable performance with an Old Vic Phaedra (21 11 84) directed by Philip Prowse in a new translation by Robert David MacDonald. Judi Dench charted a similar journey from modern dress to revered classical role. Her miraculously understated performance in Hugh Whitemore's *Pack of Lies* – a decent, enthralling West End play – was followed by an intriguing Mother Courage with the RSC at the Barbican (7 11 84).

Other artists we should celebrate in this thespian year are Alec Guinness as a finical, sympathetic Shylock at Chichester, Janet Suzman as Fugard's Lena at Hampstead, Rowan Atkinson nervelessly nerdish and extremely funny at the Aldwych, and the entire cast of William Gaskill's exemplary *The Way of the World* at Chichester (1 8 84), probably the best line-up of the year: Maggie Smith, Joan Plowright, Ian Hogg, Michael Jayston, John Moffatt, James Villiers, Sara Kestelman, Sheila Allen, Jane Carr . . . no subsidised house could match that lot, and the majority of them later trooped majestically into the Haymarket (13 11 84).

In such a year, the profession's losses were more poignant than ever. The comic muse was particularly offended by the untimely departures of Leonard Rossiter, Eric Morecambe and Tommy Cooper. Dame Flora Robson slipped quietly away aged 82, while Richard Burton was noisily and generously remembered, having just completed what proved to be one of his most effective film performances in, as it happens, *1984*.

Actors need to be seen, and to be seen they have to be lit. The death of lighting designer Joe Davis – in this theatre year he worked on *The Aspern Papers* and *42nd Street* – was a jolting reminder of his immense contribution. He was father figure to all of our distinguished artists of the spotlight and computerised board, the first to gain proper recognition within the theatre for a design skill so often and most easily taken for granted by audiences. He leaves behind a legacy of talent and accomplishment in the comparatively unheralded work of those whom he helped and influenced: Richard Pilbrow, Leonard Tucker, Robert Ornbo, Andy Phillips, David Hersey, Nick Chelton, Mick Hughes, Chris Ellis, Brian Harris and all who cast illumination upon sets, plays and, especially, actors.

All the World's a Stage...

but preferably across not more than two columns
By Donald Cooper

Do you ever wonder why theatre photographs appear as they do? Have you noticed how rarely you see full-stage, or even large group, shots? Is the selection of photographs in *Theatre Year* a puzzle to you? Let me explain the whys and wherefores of theatre photography in London, and at the same time argue the case for better photographic facilities.

Every year in London (for this purpose an area bounded by Croydon and Watford, Hammersmith and Stratford East) there are around three to four hundred new theatre productions (not including opera and ballet). Virtually all of these have their own production photographer, most hold Press photocalls, and the photographs you see derive from one or other source.

There are about a dozen freelances specialising in stage photography (some of whom also cover opera and ballet), and although we are strictly speaking competitors, there are unwritten, gentlemanly guidelines which apply for most of the time as to operational territories. Some only do production work (known as 'Front of House', or FOH for short), some only 'service' the Press, and the rest, like myself, do both.

The national newspapers which publish photographs to accompany reviews (principally *The Times, The Guardian,* the *Financial Times*, the *Daily Telegraph* and – since we are really talking about the coverage of London theatre – *The Standard*) rely on particular freelances to supply them with unique photographs, which will not, in theory, appear in a rival paper on the same day, or even worse, previously. It is this notion of exclusivity which maintains the freelance phalanx, although it is often debatable just how different the photographic results from a posed photocall can be. Dress rehearsals at least give us an opportunity to capture a wider variety of images and to supply prints more suited to the needs and preferences of each newspaper.

Fleet Street's traditional demand for tightly composed photographs with as little black (background) as possible does influence the way we shoot dress rehearsals or tackle photocalls. At the former we can usually choose our vantage point and make use of a variety of lenses to achieve the desired images. At the latter we can alter the lighting and staging which often makes sense so long as we do not in the process destroy the unique visual interest (if any) of the production, or unsettle the cast by describing as unworkable the presentation that has evolved through patient weeks of rehearsal. We have to be careful of our phrasing: muttering 'It doesn't make' at this sensitive point en route to the first night – often only a day away – does nothing to induce confidence. Neither does wholesale condemnation of the lighting which may well be adequate dramatically speaking, but problematical from our point of view. And there is a real danger in re-jigging all photocalls to suit, for example, *The Guardian*'s apparent passion for single-column photographs. How much can you say about any production within such a restrictive format?

This is the big difference in approach between Press and FOH photography. Theatre managements need the compact close-ups of well-known performers demanded by Fleet Street, for free distribution to publications which do not buy in material, but they also want a comprehensive record, to give an overall impression of a production and to ensure that everyone in the cast is covered. Normally the production photographer will have a dress rehearsal to shoot through, or a special photocall. Occasionally there will be both, or the Press photocall can double up as a second opportunity. Where practicable we will watch rehearsals prior to the final run, but unless the staging is complete and the lighting states are finalised, it isn't always very helpful. You will probably save film because you know where to concentrate your efforts, but many cuts and changes can occur before the final dress rehearsal, leaving you thoroughly disorientated by axed landmarks.

Only the RSC, as a matter of policy, invites the production photographer and the Press to dress rehearsals of all its new productions (and London transfers). The NT frequently banishes even the production photographer to a sound-proof box at the back of the Olivier and Lyttelton stalls to concentrate mightily through a 300mm f2.8 lens and achieve those increasingly familiar shots of vertiginous perspective. *Venice Preserv'd* was the only NT production in the last year offered to the Press as a dress rehearsal, and for *Wild Honey* we were only given Act I. Those who have seen the play, will appreciate that this was the least interesting photographically, and for whatever the reasons behind that decision, it left us with an impoverished record of a good and important production. It is very much in the theatre's interest – every theatre – to help secure the best possible photographs for publication, without giving away the plot or visual surprises.

As photographers we have to be aware of the problems as seen by the other side. A dozen SLR's going off more or less simultaneously during dress rehearsals can be distracting (especially in small theatres like Hampstead, or even the Royal Court, both of whose productions deserve better photographic coverage than they usually get). Photocalls are frequently scheduled at a time in the production schedule when everybody would much rather be getting on with rehearsals, especially if the going is tough. Sometimes we are semi-unwelcome interlopers, a necessary evil to be catered for as part and parcel of putting a production together.

This is where the public relations officer (PR) is particularly important. Usually a member of staff in the subsidised companies, or a freelance in the commercial field, she (it is predominantly a female province, with a few notable exceptions) will be in a prime position to influence events. Good photographs published editorially are the publicity equal of a great many paid-for column inches of advertising, and PRs understand the value and importance of this.

PRs are involved right from the start in the whole process of launching a production, and since they have to work closely together, often have a say in the choice of production photographer. Other factors affecting the choice include previous acquaintance or working experience with the producer, director or leading actors, suitability of photographic style, reliability, and fee level: more often than not, though, it is who you know that matters, rather than how good or expensive you are.

Amongst all the other tasks to be organised – interviews, Press releases, advertising – a photocall will be high on the PR's agenda. It has to be timed to fit in with the production schedule, to catch publication deadlines, and to avoid clashing with other calls or rehearsals. When it comes to choosing the shots, all kinds of considerations come into play. There may be aspects of the production which need to be kept secret to preserve their impact during performance. It may be technically difficult or too time-consuming to change sets or costumes within the time allocated, and it can even be a case of making do with whatever, and whoever, is available at that point in rehearsals.

Moments which seem visually interesting to the director could well strike us as less so (the duel in *Hamlet*, or the balcony scene in *Romeo and Juliet* are good examples, if only because of the news-paper parameters of tightness and brightness). And the under-standable desire to include everyone should be resisted whenever it dilutes the overall potential visual impact of the photocall.

Too many photocalls are overambitious, trying to present lots of snippets covering as many people as possible. Whilst we need some variety to minimise duplication of published images, it is generally better to concentrate on a few really good scenes and be prepared to repeat them until the photographers are satisfied that they have captured something worthwhile. We are not usually familiar with the play, and depend entirely on a wise selection of scenes and strong directorial guidance to realise them effectively. Directors who wash their hands of photocalls beforehand stand to wring them over the results afterwards. PRs, likewise, have to be prepared to involve themselves at photocalls and to act as intermediaries between the Press and the company, and to keep everything running smoothly. (They also rustle up coffee when the customary delays become embarrassing, or even champagne: it has been known!)

The deadlines in production photography are always very short, since the sets, costumes, wigs and – most importantly – the lighting are rarely ready before the (last) dress rehearsal before previews start, and then it is a race to supply all the necessary prints by the first night. Most photographers and PRs would agree that it is a relief to know that the workload of ordering, printing, captioning and distributing Press prints is greatly reduced by freelances, at their own expense in terms of materials and time, servicing the requirements of their regular outlets.

Even if the production photographer does have a better selection of photographs, thanks to superior facilities, it is more than likely that the photographs accompanying the reviews will be by freelances, however good or bad the Press photocall was.

It all boils down to a question of priorities. How important are good photographs in terms of immediate publicity, FOH display and as a long-term record? If the answer is 'not very' then the inevitable decline in facilities follows. Dress rehearsals are closed to just the production photographer (some of whom claim this is necessary for them to function properly, although open rehearsals seem to yield equally good results) and photocalls are cobbled together as a matter of expediency. Frequently the whole company is called, although everybody knows that in all probability only photographs of the principals stand a chance of being published.

Essentially, theatre photography is a matter of record, of capturing what is presented to us, whether at a run or a photocall. But there is an interpretative element which is pretty well removed at photocalls, especially when we do not know the production. We have to take what we are offered in good faith, whether it is truly representative or interesting, or not: how can we tell? There is a temptation for the cast not to act, not to 'play out', yet the diminish-ing effect of still photography actually demands a real effort in terms of performance in order that the final result does not look lifeless. All theatres want good, exciting photographs to send out for publicity, to put bottoms on seats essentially, and yet the means to achieve these are frequently lacking.

Whilst mediocre productions stand to yield only mediocre photographs, a number of generally acclaimed plays have managed no better (*Pack of Lies, Tom and Viv* amongst those included in this edition, *The Biko Inquest, Sufficient Carbohydrate* and *The Country Girl* amongst those excluded). West End musicals often afford us dress rehearsals, but for every *42nd Street* there is a *Dear Anyone*, and *Starlight Express* was in a category of its own, naturally, with more photographers than rollerskaters at the photocall. The resulting unanimated photographs couldn't begin to do justice to the production in terms of its visual excitement, but nobody can say in this instance that the photographs were not used, or that the production received no publicity.

I have often reflected, as we severally trek from call to call through rain-swept traffic jams, that the true sign of a free, democratic Press is really this seemingly ludicrous overkill of so many skilled people churning out basically similar, frequently undistinguished work which could be obtained for gratis, all in the name of exclusivity and freedom of choice. How lucky we are! And yet, how silly not to maximise the potential advantages of the system. Perhaps the newspapers should stand behind us more often (or even at all) and demand decent photographic facilities instead of tolerating some of the results of what we are offered.

If producers want to present their product in the best possible way they must give careful thought to each and every photocall. If photography is important, treat it accordingly. Don't leave photo-calls to organise themselves: they never do. Be realistic about what will succeed, and concentrate on it. If a picture is worth a thousand words, and a photograph accompanying a good review probably is, then it is worth setting out to obtain photographs that will be published, preferably prominently. Why settle for less than the best? Then fewer productions will be cast aside on the grounds of visual mediocrity when *Theatre Year* is being compiled, and it really will become a record of the best, most interesting productions – not just the best photographed.

1　Jack Shepherd *Richard Roma*; Tony Haygarth *James Lingk*

Glengarry Glen Ross　Cottesloe　21 9 83

2 John Matshikiza; Noni Hazlehurst; Gary Olsen

Cut & Thrust The Drill Hall 28 9 83

3 Liza Goddard *Jo*; Philip Bird *Stewart*; Stephen Moore *Toby*; Glyn Owen *John*

The Hard Shoulder Aldwych 3 10 83

4 Juliet Stevenson *Isabella*; Daniel Massey *Vincentio*; David Schofield *Angelo*

Measure for Measure Royal Shakespeare Theatre, Stratford 4 10 83

5 Richard Griffiths *Volpone*; Gemma Jones *Lady Politic Would-Be*

Volpone The Other Place 5 10 83

6 Diana Quick *Anna*; Hywel Bennett *Tim*

Fly Away Home Lyric Hammersmith Studio 10 10 83

7 Kathryn Pogson *Rowena*; Patti Love *Hilary*

8 *Audrey II*; Ellen Greene *Audrey*

9 Leslie Phillips *Gayev*; Joan Plowright *Madame Ranevskaya*; Joanna David *Varya*

The Cherry Orchard Theatre Royal, Haymarket 18 10 83

10 Michael Matou *Theseus/Oberon*; Lindsay Kemp *Puck*

A Midsummer Night's Dream Sadler's Wells 18 10 83

11 Sinead Cusack *Daisy Bone*

The Custom of the Country The Pit 19 10 83

12 Bob Peck *Pavel Lermontov*

13 Antony Sher *Martin Glass*

Maydays Barbican 20 10 83

14 Simon Callow *Sir Novelty Fashion*; Chas Bryer *Foretop*

The Relapse Lyric Hammersmith 24 10 83

15 Lindsay Kemp *Nijinsky*

Nijinsky The Fool Sadler's Wells 24 10 83

16 Rosalyn Landor *Sorel Bliss*; Penelope Keith *Judith Bliss*; Mark Payton *Simon Bliss*

Hay Fever Queen's 26 10 83

17 Michael Williams *Bob Jackson*; Judi Dench *Barbara Jackson*; Eva Griffith *Julie Jackson*; Richard Vernon *Mr Stewart*

18 centre rear: Kenneth Branagh *Francis*

Francis Greenwich 27 10 83

19 Jane Carr *Alicia*; Paul Eddington *Albert*; Georgina Hale *Cheryl*; Colin Blakely *George*

Lovers Dancing Albery 27 10 83

20 Gerard Murphy *Pericles*; Brian Protheroe *Antiochus*

Pericles Theatre Royal, Stratford East 31 10 83

21 Tracey Ullman *Carmen*; Ron Cook *Andre*; Alan Rickman *Dennis*

The Grass Widow Royal Court 1 11 83

22 David Threlfall *Apoo*; Carol Leader *Ibis*

23 Jane Lapotaire *Mercedes*

Dear Anyone Cambridge 8 11 83

24 John Price *Dorante*; Holly Wilson *Araminte*

False Admissions Lyric Hammersmith Studio 8 11 83

25 Sandra Voe *The Marquise*; Holly Wilson *The Comtesse*; Maggie Wells *Lisette*; Sam Dale *Arlequin*; Philip Voss *The Chevalier*

Successful Strategies Lyric Hammersmith Studio 15 11 83

26 Paul Nicholas *Blondel*; the Blondettes

Blondel Old Vic 9 11 83

27

Dancin' Theatre Royal Drury Lane 14 11 83

28 Antonia Ellis *Dick Whittington*; Alfred Marks *Obadiah Upward*; Geoffrey Hutchings *Lady Dodo*

Poppy Adelphi 22 11 83

29 Omar Sharif *HRH, The Grand Duke Charles*; Debbie Arnold *Miss Mary Morgan*

The Sleeping Prince Theatre Royal, Haymarket 24 11 83

30 Ramolao Makhene *Willie*; Duart Sylwain *Hally*; John Kani *Sam*

Master Harold . . . and the Boys Cottesloe 24 11 83

31 Miles Anderson *Sigismund*

Life's A Dream The Other Place 30 11 83

32 Kelly Hunter *Young Jean*

Jean Seberg Olivier 1 12 83

33 Gary Waldhorn *Martin*; Geraldine James *Sally*; Peter Jonfield *Keith*; Frances Barber *Penny*; Charles Dance *Frank*

Turning Over Bush 9 12 83

34 Elaine Paige *Carabosse*

Abbacadabra Lyric Hammersmith 13 12 83

35 Derek Newark *Gloria*; Robert Stephens *Euphoria*

36 Susan Fleetwood *Prince Charming*

Cinderella Lyttelton 15 12 83

37 Danny La Rue *Mrs Dolly Gallagher Levi*

Hello, Dolly! Prince of Wales 3184

38 John Carlisle *Minister*; Ian Talbot *Pierre*; Bill Stewart *Headmaster*; Geoffrey Freshwater *Vidocq*; Pip Miller; Phillip Walsh; Hepburn Graham; Christopher Bowen; Brian Parr; Malcolm Storry *Lacenaire*

39 Timothy West *Stalin*; Peter Kelly *Prokofiev*; Jonathan Adams *Zhdanov*; David Bamber *Shostakovich*

40 Michael Pennington *Strider*; Dinah Stabb *Vyazopurikha*

Strider – The Story of a Horse Cottesloe 26 1 84

41 Rupert Everett *Flamineo*; Ann Mitchell *Cornelia*

The White Devil Greenwich 2 2 84

42 Stevan Rimkus *Phil MacFerson*; Kenny Ireland *Eddie*

Rents Lyric Hammersmith 7 2 84

43 Tom Wilkinson *Tom*; Julie Covington *Viv*

Tom and Viv Royal Court 8 2 84

44 Peter Blake *The Intruder*; Michael Denison *The Bishop of Lax*; Royce Mills
The Reverend Lionel Toop; Derek Nimmo *The Reverend Arthur Humphrey*;
Christopher Timothy *Lance Corporal Clive Winton*

See How They Run Shaftesbury 14 2 84

45 Frances de la Tour *Joan*

Saint Joan Olivier 16 2 84

46 Janet Suzman *Lena*; Stuart Wilson *Boesman*

Boesman and Lena Hampstead Theatre 22 2 84

47 Duncan Preston *Harold Mitchell*; Sheila Gish *Blanche Du Bois*

A Streetcar Named Desire Mermaid 28 2 84

48 Karen Wood *Pitti-Sing*; Marie Baron *Yum-Yum*; Karen Skidmore *Peep-Bo*

The Mikado Old Vic 29 2 84

49 Vanessa Redgrave *Miss Tina*; Christopher Reeve *Henry Jarvis*;
Wendy Hiller *Miss Juliana Bordereau*

The Aspern Papers Theatre Royal, Haymarket 8 3 84

50 Paul McGann *Dennis*; Neil Pearson *Hal*; Leonard Rossiter *Truscott*; Patrick O'Connell *McLeavy*; Gemma Craven *Fay*

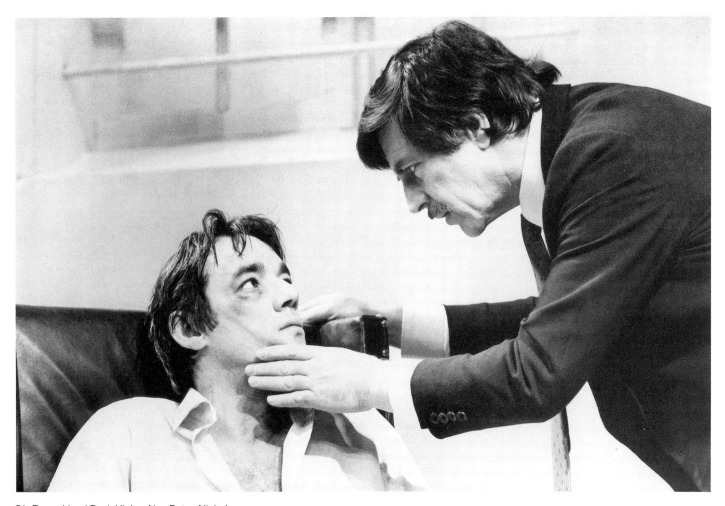

51 Roger Lloyd Pack *Victor*; Alan Bates *Nicholas*

One for the Road Lyric Hammersmith Studio 15 3 84

52 Jeff Shankley *Greaseball*

53 Frances Ruffelle *Dinah*; Chrissy Wickham *Ashley*; Stephanie Lawrence *Pearl*; Ray Shell *Rusty*

54 Jeffrey Daniel *Electra*; Voyd *Volta*

Starlight Express Apollo Victoria 27 3 84

55 Kenneth Branagh *King Henry V*; Cécile Paoli *Katharine*

Henry V Royal Shakespeare Theatre, Stratford 28 3 84

56 Simon Templeman *Robin Starveling*; Frank Middlemass *Peter Quince*; George Raistrick *Tom Snout*; Andrew Hall *Francis Flute*;
Philip Jackson *Nick Bottom*

A Midsummer Night's Dream The Other Place 29 3 84

57 Souad Faress *Sita*; Dev Sagoo *Harold*

The Great Celestial Cow Royal Court 3 4 84

58 Patricia Hodge *Jane*; Oliver Cotton *David*; Brenda Blethyn *Sheila*; Tim Pigott-Smith *Colin*

Benefactors Vaudeville 4 4 84

59 Glenda Jackson *Nina Leeds*; Edward Petherbridge *Charles Marsden*

Strange Interlude Duke of York's 6 4 84

60 Frances Tomelty *Portia*; Richard Easton *Duke of Venice*; Ian McDiarmid *Shylock*; Christopher Ravenscroft *Antonio*

The Merchant of Venice Royal Shakespeare Theatre, Stratford 10 4 84

61 Frances Barber *Marguerite Gautier*; Nicholas Farrell *Armand Duval*

Camille The Other Place 11 4 84

62 Ian McKellen *Pierre*

63 Jane Lapotaire *Belvidera*; Michael Pennington *Jaffier*

Venice Preserv'd Lyttelton 12 4 84

64 Patrick Barlow *Desmond Olivier Dingle*; Jim Broadbent *Wallace*;
Andrea Durant *Miss Durant*

The Complete Guide to Sex Lyric Hammersmith 13 4 84

65 Kenny Ireland *Old Major*; Greg Hicks *Snowball*;
David Ryall *Squealer*

66 Barrie Rutter *Napoleon*

67 Amanda Root *Juliet*; Polly James *Nurse*

68 Roger Rees *David*; Leo Wringer *Victor*

Cries From The Mammal House Royal Court 5 5 84

69 Simon Callow *Tony Perelli*; Sayo Inaba *Akiko*

On The Spot Duke of York's 9 5 84

70 Jackie Smith-Wood *Eliza Doolittle*; Peter O'Toole *Professor Higgins*

Pygmalion Shaftesbury 15 5 84

71 Jan Hartley *Maria*; Steven Pacey *Tony*

West Side Story Her Majesty's 16 5 84

72 Jane Lapotaire *Antigone*

Antigone Cottesloe 17 5 84

73 Trevor Ray *Roxy Gottlieb*; Jeremy Flynn *Joe Bonaparte*; Lisa Eichhorn *Lorna Moon*

74 Max Wall *Bludgeon*; Albert Finney *Serjeant Musgrave*

Serjeant Musgrave's Dance Old Vic 23 5 84

75 Russ Abbot *Amos Pinchley*; Sheila White *Belle*

Little Me Prince of Wales 30 5 84

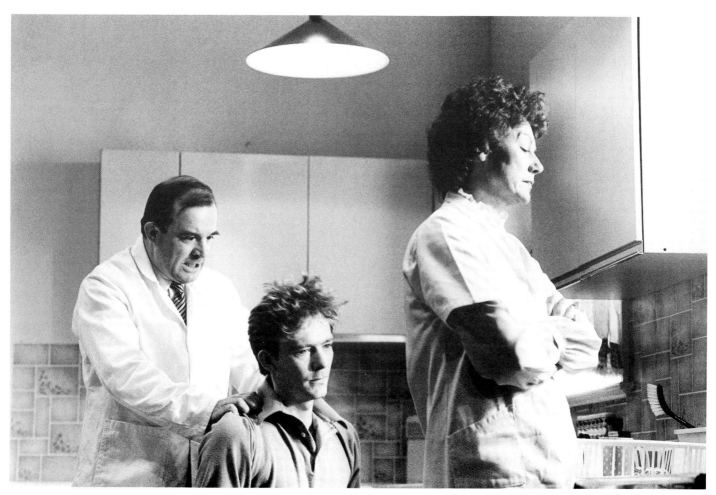

76 John Joyce *Father*; Rob Dixon *Son*; Gillian Barge *Mother*

Delicatessen Half Moon 11 6 84

77 Robin Herford *Toby*; Lavinia Bertram *Celia*

Intimate Exchanges Greenwich 11 6 84

78 Tim Flavin *Phil Dolan III, Junior*; Natalia Makarova *Vera Baronova*

On Your Toes Palace 12 6 84

79 John Savident *Nicia*; Timothy Spall *Ligurio*

Mandragola Olivier 14 6 84

80 Antony Sher *Richard III*

Richard III Royal Shakespeare Theatre, Stratford 19 6 84

81 Josette Simon *Dorcas*

Golden Girls The Other Place 20 6 84

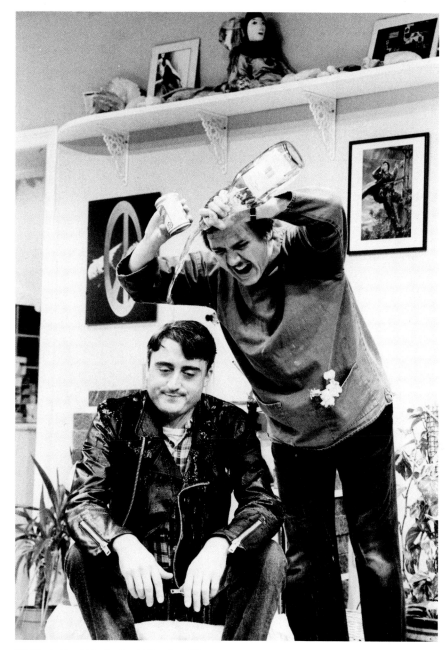

82 Kevin Elyot *Martin*; David Bamber *Oliver*

83 Clive Francis *Humphry*; Robert East *Nick*; Ian Ogilvy *Martin*; Simon Williams *Peter*

The Common Pursuit Lyric Hammersmith 3 7 84

84 Michael Pennington *Anton Chekhov*

Anton Chekhov Cottesloe 5 7 84

85 Kathryn Pogson *Leticia Bredwell*; Alan Rickman *Gayman*; Mark Tandy *Bredwell*; Pam Ferris *Parson*; Denis Lawson *Bellmour*;
Harriet Walter *Lady Julia Fulbank*

The Lucky Chance Royal Court 10 7 84

86 Alec Guinness *Shylock*

The Merchant of Venice Chichester Festival Theatre 11 7 84

87 Anna Quayle *Madame Dubonnet*; Derek Waring *Percival Browne*

The Boyfriend Old Vic 18 7 84

88 Ian McKellen *Platonov*; Elizabeth Garvie *Sofya*

Wild Honey Lyttelton 19 7 84

89 John Cater *Godfrey Pond*; Jane Booker *Joyce Harper*; Maria Aitken *Miss Gossage*; Peggy Mount *Miss Evelyn Whitchurch*;
Richard O'Callaghan *Rupert Billings*; Paul Greenwood *Dick Tassell*

The Happiest Days of Your Life Barbican 24 7 84

90 Richard Griffiths *Nikolai*; David Schofield *Lubzin*

Red Star The Pit 25 7 84

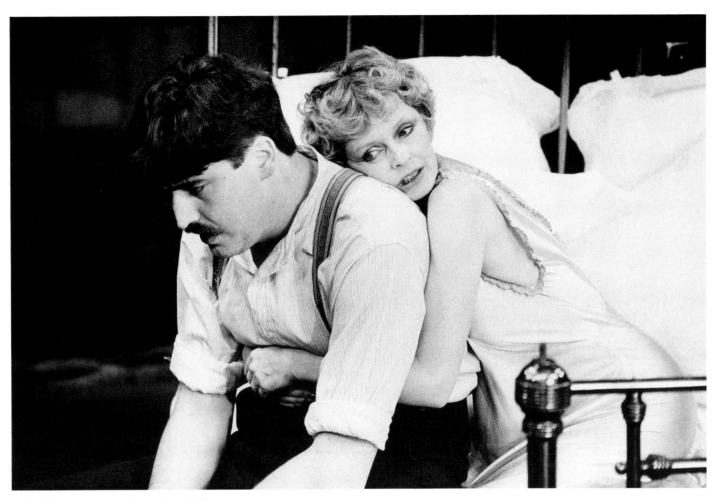

91   Alfred Molina *Alfredo*; Morag Hood *Julia*

A Little Like Drowning Hampstead Theatre 26 7 84

92 Al Pacino *Walter Cole*

American Buffalo Duke of York's 2 8 84

93 Michael Howe *Billy Lawlor*; Clare Leach *Peggy Sawyer*

42nd Street Theatre Royal, Drury Lane 8 8 84

94 Graeme Garden *Benoit Pinglet*; Deborah Norton *Angelique Pinglet*

A Little Hotel on the Side Olivier 9 8 84

95 Paul Eddington *Headmaster*

Forty Years On Queen's 13 8 84

96 Marcel Marceau *Bip*

Marcel Marceau Old Vic 20 8 84

97 Peter McEnery *Urbain Grandier*; Estelle Kohler *Sister Jeanne of the Angels*

The Devils The Pit 23 8 84

98 Ian McDiarmid *John Tagg*; David Threlfall *Joe Shawcross*

The Party The Other Place 29 8 84

99 Frank Grimes *Christopher Mahon*; Kevin Lloyd *Shawn Keogh*; Carolyn Pickles *Margaret Flaherty*

The Playboy of the Western World Riverside 30 8 84

100 Brian Cox *Detective Inspector Nelson*; Gary Oldman *Constable Naylor*

Rat in the Skull Royal Court 4 9 84

101 Frank Middlemass *Polonius*; Roger Rees *Hamlet*; Dexter Fletcher *Second Player*; Stephen Simms *Third Player*; Derek Crewe *Fourth Player*; Bernard Horsfall *First Player*

102 Frances Barber *Ophelia*; Roger Rees

Hamlet Royal Shakespeare Theatre, Stratford 5 9 84

103 Gerard Murphy *Goetz*

The Devil and the Good Lord Lyric Hammersmith 13 9 84

104 Gabrielle Lord *Andy*; Marcia Warren *Vera*; Barbara Ferris *Mavis*; Barbara Young *Maxine*; Diane Langton *Sylvia*; Josephine Gordon *Dorothy*

105 Rowan Atkinson *Rick Steadman*

The Nerd Aldwych 3 10 84

106 Ian Charleson *Eddie*; Julie Walters *May*

Fool for Love Cottesloe 4 10 84

107 Roger Rees *Berowne*

Love's Labour's Lost Royal Shakespeare Theatre, Stratford 10 10 84

108 Felicity Dean *Janet Hole*; Richard Wilson *Sir Walter Pursar*

An Honourable Trade Royal Court 16 10 84

109 Mark Hadfield *Stan Laurel*; Kenneth H. Waller *Oliver Hardy*

Blockheads Mermaid 18 10 84

110 Alun Armstrong *Leontes*; Lynn Farleigh *Hermione*

The Winter's Tale RSC/Nat West Tour August-December 1984

111 Caroline Milmoe *Betty Parris*; Jenifer Landor *Abigail Williams*

The Crucible RSC/Nat West Tour August-December 1984

Index 1
Production notes
Compiled by Michael Coveney

1 **Glengarry Glen Ross** by David Mamet. Directed by Bill Bryden, designed by Hayden Griffin, lighting by Andy Phillips. Stooge outsider blinded by the science of sale-speak in world première of a brilliant piece staged by Mamet's same NT team for *American Buffalo* in 1978.

2 **Cut and Thrust Cabaret** devised and directed by Robyn Archer. Presented by Silver Lining in association with the Drill Hall. Designed by David Blight, musical direction by Andrew Bell. Mixed bag political cabaret, Australian actress Noni Hazlehurst scoring with an atom bomb calypso à la Carmen Miranda.

3 **The Hard Shoulder** by Stephen Fagan. Presented by Michael Codron, directed by Nancy Meckler, designed by Tanya McCallin, costumes by Sheelagh Killeen, lighting by Robert Ornbo. Modest, neat comedy among the Volvo-driving architects and planners of North London. Hampstead Theatre (21 10 82) transfer.

4 **Measure for Measure** by Shakespeare. Directed by Adrian Noble, designed by Bob Crowley, lighting by Robert Bryan, music by Ilona Sekacz.

5 **Volpone** by Ben Jonson. Directed by Bill Alexander, designed by Alison Chitty, music by Guy Woolfenden, lighting by Leo Leibovici.

6 **Fly Away Home** by William Humble. Directed by Peter James, designed by Roger Glossop, lighting by Dave Horn. Notable cast in promising first play of yet more marital bickering over lifestyle and unwanted children.

7 **Masterpieces** by Sarah Daniels. Directed by Jules Wright, designed by David Roger, costumes by Di Seymour. Vigorous attack on pornography, scenes of feminist awakening in a play which, by the end of the theatre year, had become much performed all over the country. Patti Love's monologue of remembered adolescent sex and contraception adventures was one of the year's best and funniest speeches.

8 **Little Shop of Horrors** by Howard Ashman (book and lyrics) and Alan Menken (music) based on the film by Roger Corman. Presented by Cameron Mackintosh, David Geffen, the Shubert Organisation and the WPA Theatre, directed by Howard Ashman, designed by Edward T Gianfrancesco and Tim Goodchild, choreography by Edie Cowan, lighting by David Hersey, musical direction by Roger Ward, sound by Martin Levan. Ellen Greene's lisping, wilting flower proved no match for the voracious prickly pear heroine of a tacky rocky horror show.

9 **The Cherry Orchard** by Chekhov. Presented by Duncan C Weldon with Paul Gregg and Lionel Becker for Triumph Apollo Productions, directed by Lindsay Anderson, designed by Kenneth Mellor, costumes by Mark Negin, lighting by Andy Phillips. Decent revival, first seen at the 1983 Edinburgh Festival, Leslie Phillips showing more of himself, and to good effect, than is usually reflected in the surface gloss of a distinguished farceur.

10 **A Midsummer Night's Dream** after Shakespeare. Devised and directed by Lindsay Kemp with David Haughton, music by Carlos Miranda, costumes by Lolita and Catherine Hill, lighting by John Spradbery. The Lindsay Kemp style of intoxicated sensuality here included Italian clowns, bisexual lovers, nudity, Thisbe on stilts, and lots of glitter and tinsel.

11 **The Custom of the Country** by Nicholas Wright after John Fletcher and Philip Massinger. Directed by David Jones, designed by Ralph Koltai, music by Nigel Hess, lighting by Michael Calf. Brave but strenuous attempt to transform a Jacobean model into a Victorian look at the cultural and political roots of South Africa. Exotic, energetic, but a little recherché.

12/13 **Maydays** by David Edgar. Directed by Ron Daniels, designed by John Gunter, costumes by Di Seymour, music by Stephen Oliver, lighting by Chris Ellis. Magnificent, dialectical, objective and lushly presented political drama.

14 **The Relapse** by Vanbrugh. Directed by William Gaskill, designed by Sally Jacobs, costumes by Kandis Cook, music by Roderick Skeaping, lighting by Andy Phillips. Restoration work of the true Gaskill vintage was to come later on at Chichester, but Callow ran riot with Vanbrugh's vowels having just acquired his title for 'ten thawsand pawnd'.

15 **Nijinsky the Fool** devised and directed by Lindsay Kemp with Carlos Miranda and David Haughton. Kemp's Nijinsky was a dream-struck doll manipulated by the puppeteer Diaghilev. It was prefaced by Walton's *Façade* imaginatively staged as an Edwardian family picnic.

16 **Hay Fever** by Noël Coward. Presented by Peter Baldwin, by arrangement with Stoll Moss Theatres and Pencon Productions. Directed by Kim Grant, designed by Carl Toms, lighting by Joe Davis. Penelope Keith was quick, bossy, funny and altogether perfect casting as Judith Bliss. The setting of baronial and Georgian splendour was not right (the Blisses inhabit a cramped Thames-side cottage), the support casting uneven. The production re-couped its costs in two weeks, a West End record.

17 **Pack of Lies** by Hugh Whitemore. Presented by Michael Redington in association with Bernard Sandler and Eddie Kulukundis. Directed by Clifford Williams, designed by Ralph Koltai, lighting by Robert Ornbo. Notorious 1960 spy case with Judi Dench, understated and moving, as the suburban neighbour confusedly assisting intelligence operations. Low-key but gripping drama.

18 **Francis** by Julian Mitchell. Directed by David William, designed by Stephanie Howard, lighting by Brian Harris. The author of *Another Country* moved, with a resounding thud, from one enclosed male society to another. Kenneth Branagh's robust Francis of Assisi was strictly for the birds, his saintliness sorely tried by a company of leaping friars and a text of plummeting banality.

19 **Lovers Dancing** by Charles Dyer. Presented by Doris Cole Abrahams and Leon Becker for Albion Productions by arrangement with Ian B Albery. Directed by Donald McWhinnie, designed by Peter Rice, lighting by Leonard Tucker. A ritzy cast in a notable flop, a trite old confection of sexual and conversational arabesques executed by two married couples on the anniversary of a ballroom dancing contest. Thunderously unfunny.

20 **Pericles** by Shakespeare. Directed and designed by Ultz, music by Martin Duncan, lighting by Mick Hughes. Excitingly, inventively pantomimed production with Gerard Murphy embarking on the final leg of his trip to stardom. Low budget proved no obstacle to imaginative ideas. Delightful.

21 **The Grass Widow** by Snoo Wilson. Directed by Max Stafford-Clark, designed by Peter Hartwell, costumes by Pam Tait, lighting by Robin Myerscough-Walker. Hippie hangovers on a Californian dope farm where a dead dealer's creditors and friends roll up to inhale each other. Not one of Wilson's best, a bit of a mish-hash in fact.

22 **Topokana Martyrs' Day** by Jonathan Falla. Directed by Simon Stokes, designed by Geoff Rose, lighting by Bart Cossee. Little light famine relief at an East African aid centre. Notable début by writer using his experience to point up the good and bad intentions of white charity workers.

23 **Dear Anyone** by Don Black (lyrics), Geoff Stephens (music) and Jack Rosenthal (book). Birmingham Rep production presented by Triumph Apollo and MAM in association with David Susskind and the Dick James Organisation. Directed by David Taylor, designed by Ralph Koltai and Nadine Baylis, choreography by Tudor Davies, musical direction by Chris Walker, lighting by Benny Ball, sound by Jonathan Deans. Dire, imitation American musical with Jane Lapotaire as an agony aunt with problems of her own, many of them starting with the music and lyrics. Fine steel-plated astrolabè setting for the *New York Globe*.

24/25 **False Admissions** and **Successful Strategies** by Marivaux, translated by Timberlake Wertenbaker. Presented by Shared Experience, directed by Mike Alfreds, designed by Paul Dart. Interesting, adventurous productions of two Marivaux comedies playing in repertory.

26 **Blondel** by Tim Rice (lyrics) and Stephen Oliver (music). Presented by Cameron Mackintosh and Heartaches Productions, directed by Peter James, musical staging by Anthony van Laast, designed by Tim Goodchild, lighting by Andrew Bridge, sound by Martin Levan, orchestrations by John Cameron, musical direction by Martin Koch. Travelling minstrel with backing group on Ye Olde Toppe of Ye Olde Poppies. Surprisingly transferred for six-month run to the Aldwych (20 1 84).

27 **Dancin'** devised with choreography by Bob Fosse. Presented by Tom Arnold in association with Louis Benjamin and Peter Baldwin, restaged for London by Gail Benedict, designed by Peter Larkin, costumes by Willa Kim, lighting by Jules Fisher. Grim irony as this third-rate dance cabaret with its raucous Yankee Doodle finale opened on the very day Britain took custody of American cruise missiles at Greenham Common.

28 **Poppy** by Peter Nichols (book and lyrics) and Monty Norman (music). The RSC production presented by Michael S Landes, Burton I Litwin, Albert Schwartz, Bert Siegelson and Louise Westergaard in association with ALMI Entertainment Finance Corp, directed by Terry Hands, choreographed by Onna White, designed by Farrah, costumes by Alexander Reid, musical direction by Ian Macpherson. This Broadway-bound revival never took off, so we shall never know how New York might have responded to this mordant Victorian pantomime, largely re-cast since the Barbican (5 10 82) but with Geoffrey Hutchings repeating his splendidly coarse but controlled dame.

29 **The Sleeping Prince** by Terence Rattigan. Chichester Festival Theatre production (3 8 83) presented by Triumph Apollo in association with Proscenium Productions. Directed by Peter Coe, designed by Peter Rice, lighting by Mick Hughes. 1953 Coronation comedy of a prince and a showgirl, roles first played by Olivier and Vivien Leigh (Monroe in the film).

30 **Master Harold . . . and the Boys** by Athol Fugard. Market Theatre Company, Johannesburg, production directed by Fugard, designed by Douglas Heap, costumes by Robyn Lewis, lighting by Mannie Manim. Auto-biographical play hingeing on a confessional racist outburst by a white teenager in front of his black best friends, waiters in a 1950 Port Elizabeth tea-room. Outstanding performance by John Kani.

31 **Life's a Dream** by Calderon adapted by John Barton and Adrian Mitchell. Directed by Barton, designed by Christopher Morley, lighting by Leo Leibovici, music by Guy Woolfenden. The real horse, mounted by the urchin prince Sigismund as he abandoned romance for political responsibility, did not, alas, transfer with the rest to the Pit in the Barbican (4 5 84).

32 **Jean Seberg** by Julian Barry (book), Christopher Adler (lyrics) and Marvin Hamlisch (music). Directed by Peter Hall, designed by John Bury, choreography by Irving Davies, orchestration by Bill Byers, musical direction by Ray Cook. Failing to justify its bad pre-publicity, Hall's mask work on *The Oresteia* and *Animal Farm* had a little interim expression in the show's most tastelessly sardonic number 'It's the Least We Could Do' for Seberg and doctors in white coats.

33 **Turning Over** by Brian Thompson. Directed by David Hayman, designed by Sue Plummer, lighting by Gerry Jenkinson. Funny play, especially in the first act, about a British TV crew in India seeking firstly a good film and, secondly, the answer to Life.

34 **Abbacadabra** by Bjorn Ulvaeus and Benny Andersson (music), Alain and Daniel Boublil (story), David Wood (book), Don Black with Mike Batt and Bjorn Ulvaeus (lyrics). Presented by arrangement with Cameron Mackintosh, directed by Peter James, choreography by Anthony van Laast, designed by Jenny Tiramani, costumes by Sue Blane, lighting by Andrew Bridge, musical direction by Simon Webb. Video rock musical in a tubular steel forest, a computer-age congress between the Wizard of Oz and the Sleeping Beauty with thumpingly melodic music by ABBA composers.

35/36 **Cinderella** adapted (from what?) by Bill Bryden, Trevor Ray and the Company. Directed by Bryden, designed by William Dudley, costumes by Deirdre Clancy, musical direction by John Tams. Preciously inept and ghastly pantomime presented with a luridly frozen extravagance.

37 **Hello, Dolly!** by Jerry Herman (music and lyrics) and Michael Stewart (book). Presented by Triumph Apollo by arrangement with Bernard Delfont and Richard M Mills, directed by Peter Coe, designed by Tim Goodchild, lighting by Robert Ornbo, musical direction by Ed Coleman. Critically derided – and surprisingly unpopular – revival, Danny La Rue a total drag in comparison even with Carol Channing. Birmingham Rep transfer.

38 **Softcops** by Caryl Churchill. Directed by Howard Davies, designed by Bob Crowley, music by Nigel Hess. Ethereal cabaret about crime and punishment in a repressive society, with music played by the Medici String Quartet and ideas derived from Michel Foucault. Experimental all right, but unsatisfactory.

39 **Master Class** by David Pownall. Directed by Justin Greene, designed by Martin Johns, music by John White, lighting by Chris Ellis. Leicester Haymarket production, transferred to Wyndham's (28 2 84).

40 **Strider: The Story of a Horse** by Mark Rozovsky (from a story by Tolstoy), adapted and translated by Peter Tegel. Directed by Michael Bogdanov, designed by Chris Dyer, lighting by Paul McLeish, movement by David Toguri, musical direction by Terry Mortimer. More horseing around in the alternative *Equus*, a refined and seductive production.

41 **The White Devil** by John Webster. Directed and designed by Philip Prowse, lighting by Gerry Jenkinson. Opening shot in the three-play season under the guest artistic directorship of the Glasgow Citizens' Prowse. Followed by *The Way of the World* (15 3 84) and *The Seagull* (26 4 84).

42 **Rents** by Michael Wilcox. Directed by William Gaskill, designed by Dermot Hayes, lighting by Andy Phillips. Beautiful, funny revival of 1979 look at male prostitutes against the forbidding Edinburgh skyline.

43 **Tom and Viv** by Michael Hastings. Directed by Max Stafford-Clark, designed by Antony McDonald and Jock Scott, lighting by Robin Myerscough-Walker. Estrangement within T S Eliot's first marriage using the poet's own metaphor of the cage. Due for Court revival in early 1985.

44 **See How They Run** by Philip King. Presented by the Theatre of Comedy, directed by Ray Cooney, designed by Alan Miller Bunford, costumes by Joan Ellacott, lighting by James Baird. Vicars galore in classic 1945 farce.

45 **Saint Joan** by Bernard Shaw. Directed by Ronald Eyre, designed by John Gunter, lighting by Chris Ellis, music by Ilona Sekacz, sound by Chris Jordan. Unstudied, powerful Joan in an evening of rambling pageant. A very trying trial scene with an amnesiac inquisitor.

46 **Boesman and Lena** by Athol Fugard. Directed by Clare Davidson, designed by Dermot Hayes, lighting by Rory Dempster. Fine revival of 1968 portrait of South African coloureds transfixed in a severe landscape.

47 **A Streetcar Named Desire** by Tennessee Williams. Directed by Alan Strachan, designed by Bernard Culshaw, lighting by John A Williams. Sheila Gish established her star status in a superb production of the 1947 emotional roller-coaster that celebrated new ownership of the Mermaid and a guarantee of the theatre's future. Greenwich Theatre (12 9 83) transfer.

48 **The Mikado** by Gilbert and Sullivan. The Stratford, Ontario, Festival production directed by Brian MacDonald, designed by Susan Benson and Douglas McLean, lighting by Michael J Whitfield, musical direction by Berthold Carrière. Sparkish Canadian import.

49 **The Aspern Papers** adapted by Michael Redgrave from Henry James. Presented by Triumph Apollo in association with Proscenium Productions by arrangement with R&B Productions, directed by Frith Banbury, designed by Carl Toms, lighting by Joe Davis. Christopher Reeve fallible after all as the 'publishing scoundrel' who insinuates himself into the Venetian sala of a decrepit literary moll and her glowingly spinsterish niece. Redgrave outstanding in her father's 1959 play.

50 **Loot** by Joe Orton. Presented by the Theatre of Comedy, directed by Jonathan Lynn, designed by Saul Radomsky, costumes by Carrie Bayliss, lighting by Mick Hughes. Hilarious, blasphemous farce undimmed by the passage of 18 years and newly ignited by Rossiter's Clouseau-ish, gleamingly satanic Truscott of the Yard. Transferred to the Lyric (19 9 84). Rossiter, alas, collapsed during a performance on October 5 and died shortly afterwards. Dinsdale Landen succeeded him as Truscott.

51 **One for the Road** by Harold Pinter. Directed by Pinter, designed by Tim Bickerton, lighting by Dave Horn. Short lunchtime piece of interrogation and torture in an unnamed totalitarian police state. Pinter's power game moves into a more overtly political and criminal dimension. Chilling performance by Bates.

52-54 **Starlight Express** by Andrew Lloyd Webber (music) and Richard Stilgoe (lyrics). Presented by the Really Useful Theatre Company, directed by Trevor Nunn, designed by John Napier, choreography by Arlene Phillips, lighting by David Hersey, sound by Martin Levan, musical direction by David Caddick. *Cats* Mark 2 with a dash of Spielberg, *Star Wars,* Disneyland and *Rollerball.* Tremendous washes of synthesized sound, feeble narrative it would have been wiser to ditch.

55 **Henry V** by Shakespeare. Directed by Adrian Noble, designed by Bob Crowley, lighting by Robert Bryan, music by Howard Blake. Tremendous start to the new Stratford season, Branagh setting the pace.

56 **A Midsummer Night's Dream** by Shakespeare. Directed by Sheila Hancock, designed by Bob Crowley, costumes by Priscilla Truett, music by Ilona Sekacz, lighting by Brian Harris. Benignly unexceptional production arriving in Stratford after the small-scale tour of schools and colleges.

57 **The Great Celestial Cow** by Sue Townsend. Joint Stock production directed by Carole Hayman, designed by Amanda Fisk, lighting by Geoff Mersereau, choreography by Sue Lefton. Interesting, if unpolished, culture-shock play in which an Indian couple are reunited in Leicester though still separated by yards of sari and the pull of the homeland.

58 **Benefactors** by Michael Frayn. Presented by Michael Codron, directed by Michael Blakemore, designed by Michael Annals, lighting by Rory Dempster. A kitchen (less of formica than of four Michaels) is heated by the falling out of best friends, an architect and a journalist, the collapse of dreams, marriage and the high-rise apartment industry. Excellent work by Brenda Blethyn trembling on the brink then shivering in the void.

59 **Strange Interlude** by Eugene O'Neill. Presented by Triumph Apollo in association with Jerome Minskoff, directed by Keith Hack, designed by Voytek, costumes by Deirdre Clancy, lighting by Gerry Jenkinson, music by Benedict Mason. Triumphant presentation of imperfect play, Glenda Jackson crossing the years and donning an Ava Gardner turban in search of sexual and maternal fulfilment after losing her lover in the First War.

60 **The Merchant of Venice** by Shakespeare. Directed by John Caird, designed by Ultz, lighting by Robert Bryan, music by Ilona Sekacz. Controversy here over both design and performance. Ian McDiarmid replied convincingly in *The Times* to accusations of anti-semitism in his reading.

61 **Camille** by Pan Gems, adapted from *La Dame aux Camelias* by Dumas. Directed by Ron Daniels, designed by Maria Bjornson and Allan Watkins, music by Guy Woolfenden, lighting by John Waterhouse, choreography by Anthony van Laast. Unanimous applause for Frances Barber, leaping from the contemporary angst of Doug Lucie last year and Brian (Turning Over) Thompson this, to tender, tragic distinction.

62/63 **Venice Preserv'd** by Thomas Otway. Directed by Peter Gill, designed by Alison Chitty, music by Dominic Muldowney, lighting by Stephen Wentworth. Glasgow Citizens'-style designed (not *quite* convincing) and RSC-style acting still amounted to a memorable NT achievement. Should Pennington and McKellen have reversed roles, or at least alternated in them?

64 **The Complete Guide to Sex** by Patrick Barlow with Jude Kelly and Jim Broadbent. Presented by the National Theatre of Brent, directed by Kelly, designed by Kate Burnett, lighting by Dave Horn. Music hall joys 'along Brechtian lines' at the expense of sexplorers like Casanova, Michelangelo and Snow White. Broadbent, a critic's delight with the gleaming insanity of an innocent murderer, was dubbed by one 'a Scarsdale Diet Oliver Hardy'.

65/66 **Animal Farm** by Peter Hall (adaptation from George Orwell), Adrian Mitchell (lyrics) and Richard Peaslee (music). Directed by Hall, designed by Jennifer Carey, lighting by John Bury, movement by Stuart Hopps. Not a pig of a show, exactly, but as a musical it did not really go the whole hog. Transferred internally to the Olivier (27 9 84).

67 **Romeo and Juliet** by Shakespeare. Directed by John Caird, designed by Bob Crowley, costumes by Priscilla Truett, music by Ilona Sekacz, lighting by Brian Harris. Atmospheric touring production, confirming Amanda Root as one of the season's real finds.

68 **Cries from the Mammal House** by Terry Johnson. Directed by Phil Young, designed by Peter Hartwell, lighting by Richard Moffatt. Misfired anthropological comedy swinging between a South-coast zoo and darkest Mauritius. Roger Rees off-form, especially when lolling around in underpants.

69 **On the Spot** by Edgar Wallace. Presented by Freedman Panter and Namara, by arrangement with Ian B Albery. Adapted and directed by Robert Walker, designed by Patrick Robertson, costumes by Rosemary Vercoe, lighting by Mick Hughes. 1929 gangster play (the first), Callow projecting Gothic lassitude as the organ-playing lecher modelled on Al Capone. Watford Palace (7 3 84) transfer.

70 **Pygmalion** by Bernard Shaw. Presented by the Theatre of Comedy in association with the Leicester Haymarket, directed by Ray Cooney, designed by Douglas Heap, costumes by Ann Curtis, lighting by Charlie Paton. O'Toole was eccentric but impressive, exerting a bestial authority over both stage and a wide-eyed, earthy Eliza.

71 **West Side Story** by Jerome Robbins (concept and original production), Arthur Laurents (book), Leonard Bernstein (music) and Stephen Sondheim (lyrics). Leicester Haymarket production presented by Richard Pilbrow for Theatre Projects, supervised by Tom Abbott, designed by Martin Johns, lighting by Chris Ellis, musical direction by Grant Hossack. Superb, irresistible revival of 1957 classic, faithfully re-staged by Abbott.

72 **Antigone** by Sophocles, translated by C A Trypanis. Directed by John Burgess and Peter Gill, designed by Alison Chitty, lighting by Stephen Wentworth, music by Terry Davies. Lucid modern dress production, the chorus in grey suits and soft hats, Lapotaire in red dress and toque.

73 **Golden Boy** by Clifford Odets. Directed by Bill Bryden, designed by Hayden Griffin, costumes by Deirdre Clancy, lighting by Andy Phillips, music by John Tams. Underpowered revival of 1937 morality play with a boxing metaphor.

74 **Serjeant Musgrave's Dance** by John Arden. Presented by United British Artists (UBA) and Triumph Apollo, directed by Albert Finney, designed by Di Seymour, lighting by Rory Dempster, music by John Tams. Finney's mistake was to play the lead *and* to direct. The rich fruitiness of Arden's 1959 epic not harmed by Max Wall's music-hall bargee, walking up and down a bit.

75 **Little Me** by Cy Coleman (music), Carolyn Leigh (lyrics) and Neil Simon (book), based on the novel by Patrick Dennis. Presented by Bernard Delfont with Nazmu Virani by arrangement with Mike Hughes. Directed by Val May, designed by Tony Walton, lighting by Andrew Bridge, choreography by John Sharpe (from Bob Fosse's original), musical direction by Clive Chaplin. 1962 musical showing more of its age than its vintage, despite Simon's one-liners and Russ Abbot's amiability.

76 **Delicatessen** by Tilly, adapted by Derek Goldby and David Hemblen. Directed by Goldby, designed by Peter Hartwell, lighting by Andy Phillips. Weird mood piece in a food shop kitchen, spellbinding performance by Rob Dixon. 1980 French play not Anglicised with complete success.

77 **Intimate Exchanges** by Alan Ayckbourn. Directed by Ayckbourn, designed by Edward Lipscomb, lighting by Francis Lynch, music by Paul Todd. Ayckbourn's technical ingenuity is now an almost unhealthy obsession, with two skilled actors playing all the parts in a sequence of eight plays given in extended repertory. Critical and popular assessment as yet deferred as hardly anyone has bothered, or been able, to see them all. Transferred to the Ambassadors (13 8 84), presented by the Little Theatre of Comedy, five of the eight plays returning there later in the year (29 10 84).

78 **On Your Toes** by Richard Rodgers (music and book), Lorenz Hart (lyrics and book) and George Abbott (book). Presented by Michael White and the Really Useful Theatre Company Ltd, directed by Abbott and Peter Walker, designed by Zack Brown, choreography by George Balanchine, Peter Martins and Donald Saddler, lighting by John B Read, sound by Autograph, musical direction by John Mauceri and Timothy Higgs. Stylish, affectionate revival of 1936 blockbuster in which classical ballet and jazz dance meet cheek-by-jowl to whip up a storm.

79 **Mandragola** by Machiavelli, adapted by Wallace Shawn. Directed by David Gilmore, designed by Roger Glossop, lighting by David Hersey, music and lyrics by Howard Goodall. Disastrously produced, smutty update of elegant but slight sex comedy.

80 **Richard III** by Shakespeare. Directed by Bill Alexander, designed by William Dudley, music by Guy Woolfenden, lighting by Leo Leibovici, fights by Malcolm Ranson. Sher magic from a chameleon insect, crutches doubling as deadly antennae.

81 **Golden Girls** by Louise Page. Directed by Barry Kyle, designed by Kit Surrey, costumes by Allan Watkins, lighting by Wayne Dowdeswell, music by Ilona Sekacz. Sprint relay team led by Josette Simon's black gazelle. Ebulliently done.

82 **Progress** by Doug Lucie. Directed by David Hayman, designed by Geoff Rose, lighting by Bart Cossee. Pungently hilarious study of life among the trendy left.

83 **The Common Pursuit** by Simon Gray. Directed by Harold Pinter, designed by Eileen Diss, costumes by Liz Waller, lighting by Dave Horn. A group of friends travel from mid 1960s Cambridge to late 1970s literary London, losing ideals and aspirations en route.

84 **Anton Chekhov** devised by Michael Pennington. Designed by Alison Chitty, lighting by Paul McLeish. Treading gently among his own letters and stories, the modestly elusive Chekhov is here turned into a rambling old bore.

85 **The Lucky Chance** by Aphra Behn. Presented by the Women's Playhouse Trust and the Royal Court, directed by Jules Wright, designed by Jenny Tiramani, music by Ilona Sekacz, lighting by Geoffrey Joyce. Game but indecisive revival of Restoration comedy by the first professional English female writer, devious gallants helping sprightly women to deceive a pair of dilapidated, debauched and mercenary suitors.

86 **The Merchant of Venice** by Shakespeare. Directed by Patrick Garland, designed by Pamela Howard, lighting by Bill Bray, music by Christopher Littlewood. Guinness's Shylock was a trim, well-dressed, cultured and dignified figure in a production set mostly at the gates of the Jewish ghetto. Jessica's rebellion against orthodoxy made sense, but Bassanio and Antonio looked destined for each other. Here was alien dignity among the Christian corn.

87 **The Boy Friend** by Sandy Wilson. Presented by Cameron Mackintosh, directed by Christopher Hewett, designed by Robin Don, costumes by Johan Engels, choreography by Dan Siretta, lighting by Andrew Bridge, musical direction by Charles Miller. Over-blown and over-orchestrated betrayal of classic, charming 1954 parody musical. Anna Quayle's irresistibly high-camp odalisque of the plage made a change from the surrounding coarseness. Transferred to the Albery (20 9 84).

88 **Wild Honey** by Chekhov in a version by Michael Frayn. Directed by Christopher Morahan, designed by John Gunter, costumes by Deirdre Clancy, music by Dominic Muldowney, lighting by Robert Bryan. Chekhov's first play reorganised as a new-minted four-act farce. Best NT show of the year.

89 **The Happiest Days of Your Life** by John Dighton. Directed by Clifford Williams, designed by Carl Toms, lighting by Robert Bryan, music by Richard Brown. RSC dial a wrong number with a misguided, galumphingly unfunny revival of classic 1948 English farce set in a minor public school, Peggy Mount alone behaving as if to the stylistic manner born.

90 **Red Star** by Charles Wood. Directed by John Caird, designed by Chris Dyer, music by Guy Woolfenden, lighting by Michael Calf. Incoherent return to the familiar Charles Wood territory of the absurdities of film-making, this time with a bad actor imprisoned for impersonating Stalin then elevated to Soviet cinematic star status for the same crime.

91 **A Little Like Drowning** by Anthony Minghella. Directed by John Dove, designed by Tanya McCallin, costumes by Sheelagh Killeen, lighting by Mick Hughes. Touching, undemonstrative snapshot play across three generations of Anglo-Italians, Molina superb as the bear-like music-loving paterfamilias, Morag Hood the 'putana' for whom he leaves wife and children.

92 **American Buffalo** by David Mamet. The Long Wharf Theatre production presented by Duncan C Weldon with Paul Gregg and Lionel Becker, with Elliot Martin. Directed by Arvin Brown, designed by Marjorie Bradley Kellogg, costumes by Bill Walker, lighting by Ronald Wallace. Pacino's performance as a twitchy street hoodlum was a skilled exercise in riveting fidgetiness that rather dominated and then upset the sprung rhythms of Mamet's Pinteresque junk shop three-hander. The NT did it better in 1978.

93 **42nd Street** by Harry Warren (music), Al Dubin (lyrics), Michael Stewart and Mark Bramble (book), based on the novel by Bradford Ropes. Presented by David Merrick, original direction and dances by Gower Champion, directed by Lucia Victor, designed by Robin Wagner, costumes by Theoni V Aldredge, lighting by Joe Davis and Leonard Tucker from the original by Tharon Musser, musical direction by Kevin Amos, sound by Julian Beech. New York import of not all that much import, a lot of noisy dancing but little style.

94 **A Little Hotel on the Side** by Georges Feydeau and Maurice Desvallières, translated by John Mortimer. Directed by Jonathan Lynn, designed by Saul Radomsky, costumes by Alexander Reid, lighting by Mick Hughes, music by Dominic Muldowney. Better known as *Hotel Paradiso*, Mortimer's new version had some delicious jokes ('I do not care for hanky panky, frankly, Pinglet'), spirited playing by TV comic Garden, and a splendid Parisian deluge at the climax.

95 **Forty Years On** by Alan Bennett. Presented by Peter Baldwin by arrangement with Stoll Moss Theatres. Directed by Patrick Garland, designed by Peter Rice, lighting by Bill Bray, music by Christopher Littlewood. Bennett's 1968 school play parable of England in decline, stuffed full of revue sketches, literate allusions, parody and nostalgia, handsomely mounted with Paul Eddington less wispily ethereal than was Gielgud as the Headmaster, but blank, funny, beleaguered just the same. Opened Chichester Festival Theatre season (2 5 84).

96 **Marcel Marceau** presented by Theater Impresariaat Ltd in association with Food and Wine from France. As constant as the northern star, as unchanging as the Comedie Française, as predictable as *The Mousetrap*. We hear less of pure mime these days than of Dario Fo. Good thing, too. Marceau will obviously never change his act.

97 **The Devils** by John Whiting. Directed by John Barton, designed by Christopher Morley, costumes by Ann Curtis, music by Guy Woolfenden. First new play performed by the RSC (in 1961) revived without too much sexual hysteria or fanaticism. The bare bones prove less than riveting and you end up yearning guiltily for a touch of Ken Russell.

98 **The Party** by Trevor Griffiths. Directed by Howard Davies with David Edgar, designed by William Dudley, costumes by Allan Watkins, lighting by Leo Leibovici. Revival of 1973 talk-in on the state of the British left, Threlfall as the socially conscious TV producer, McDiarmid as the Glaswegian Trotskyite played at the National by Olivier. Period complement to Edgar's *Maydays*.

99 **The Playboy of the Western World** by J M Synge. Presented by UBA in association with Hiccombe Productions Ltd, directed by Lindsay Anderson, designed by Di Seymour, lighting by Andy Phillips and Jeff Beecroft. Poetic, confident revival with superb performances from Frank Grimes, Nichola McAuliffe and Carolyn Pickles. Edinburgh Festival transfer.

100 **Rat in the Skull** by Ron Hutchinson. Directed by Max Stafford-Clark, designed by Peter Hartwell, lighting by Andy Phillips. An Ulster policeman questions an IRA suspect in a London police station. Weakly resolved, the play was, nonetheless, a memorable articulation of anguish and sectarian bigotry in Northern Ireland, Brian Cox excellent as the crumpled, persistent, bulky interrogator.

101/102 **Hamlet** by Shakespeare. Directed by Ron Daniels, designed by Maria Bjornson, lighting by Chris Ellis, music by Nigel Hess, fights by Malcolm Ranson. Rees lightning strikes again in a mercurial, Bedlamite Hamlet with only Frances Barber's Ophelia and Kenneth Branagh's Laertes in the same class.

103 **The Devil and the Good Lord** by Sartre, translated by Frank Hauser. Directed by John Dexter, designed by Jocelyn Herbert, lighting by Andy Phillips. Brave, heroic, rightly acclaimed performance by Murphy in an otherwise merely efficient staging of massive philosophical 1951 play. One funny scene.

104 **Stepping Out** by Richard Harris. Presented by Bill Kenwright, directed by Julia McKenzie, designed by Stuart Stanley, lighting by Jon Swain, choreography by Tudor Davies and Jenifer Mary Morgan. Less than meets the eye in jovial amateur *Chorus Line* set in a church hall evening class. Snappy bid for stardom by Marcia Warren, funny stalwart of Ayckbourn comedies, who makes even taramasalata sound amusing. Thorndike Theatre, Leatherhead, transfer.

105 **The Nerd** by Larry Shue. Presented by Bruce Hyman and Pola Jones, directed by Mike Ockrent, designed by Roger Glossop, lighting by John B Read. Very funny low-taste show with Atkinson infinitely resourceful as the social leech who comes to dinner and is given to smelling his socks and armpits in public.

106 **Fool for Love** by Sam Shepard. Directed by Peter Gill, designed by Alison Chitty, lighting by Stephen Wentworth. Refined, over-inflected version of off-Broadway hit about incestuous jealousy on the edge of the desert.

107 **Love's Labour's Lost** by Shakespeare. Directed by Barry Kyle, designed by Bob Crowley, lighting by Chris Ellis, music by Guy Woolfenden. Nearly gorgeous, not quite intelligent revival in a French classical garden, folk music of the Navarre region and much lush literalism of interpretation: a black Rosaline ('She is born to make black fair'), archery gear and a statue of headless Cupid, scenic parasols which blossom when the sun shines.

108 **An Honourable Trade** by G F Newman. Directed by Mike Bradwell, designed by Geoff Rose, lighting by Gareth Jones. The advertising blared out promise of sex scandals in Westminster, and the private morality of people with public responsibility, hardly a new topic, was lent piquancy by the presence in the cast of a Director of Public Prosecutions, a Chairman of the Conservative Party, a Lord Chancellor and, most intriguing of all perhaps, a Chief Whip. Unluckily timed to open four days after the Brighton bombing.

109 **Blockheads** by Michael Landwehr, Kay Cole and Arthur Whitelaw (book), Hal Hackady (lyrics) and Alexander Peskanov (music). Directed by Arthur Whitelaw, choreography by Kay Cole, designed by Tim Goodchild, costumes by David Graden, lighting by Benny Ball, musical direction by Stuart Pedlar. Unnecessary Laurel and Hardy musical.

110 **The Winter's Tale** by Shakespeare. Directed by Adrian Noble, designed by Bob Crowley, costumes by David Short, music by Guy Woolfenden, lighting by Michael Calf. A wonderful RSC team led by Alun Armstrong and Lynn Farleigh, whose destroyed marriage as the Proctors in *The Crucible* found echoing, poignant complement in their renewed liaison as Leontes and Hermione. Post-war Sicilian Mediterranean feel, fine costumes for this thoroughly magical and memorable production.

111 **The Crucible** by Arthur Miller. Directed by Barry Kyle and Nick Hamm, designed by Bob Crowley, costumes by Fotini Dimou, music by Guy Woolfenden, lighting by Michael Calf. Irresistible, sweeping production with the Massachusetts puritan baroque language delivered in a ripe Warwickshire burr. The RSC NatWest tour, not remotely small scale, travelled from Scunthorpe to Darlington via Belfast and Poole with astonishingly reverberative pay-offs for this diabolic blockbuster in the cathedrals at Ripon and Lincoln. The epic and the intimate styles both flourished in a cruciform staging of platforms and tables, audience and cast for Miller and Shakespeare (see above) conjoined on a sea of Oriental carpets.

Index 2
Alphabetical list of productions

Index 3
Alphabetical list of performers